The

A -to- Z

Steps to a
Richer Life

For -
Happy Valentines Day & &
I always want you
To be happy.
I love you!
Jan &
1998 ✱

Deepak Chopra, M.D.

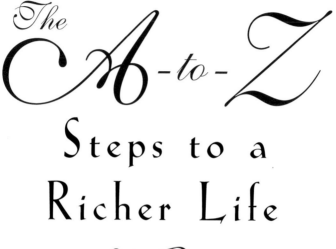

The A-to-Z Steps to a Richer Life

A Special Edition
Based on the Bestseller
Creating Affluence

BARNES & NOBLE BOOKS
NEW YORK

This edition published by Barnes & Noble, Inc.,
by arrangement with New World Library.

Copyright © 1993 by Deepak Chopra, M.D.

1994 Barnes & Noble Books

ISBN 1-56619-719-8

Book design by James Sarfati

Printed and bound in the United States of America

M 9 8 7 6 5

A NOTE
FROM THE AUTHOR

*A*FFLUENCE IS THE EXPERIENCE IN which our needs are easily met and our desires spontaneously fulfilled — whether they apply to the material realm, or to our emotional, psychological or spiritual needs, or to the realm of relationship.

A truly wealthy person's attention is never focused on money alone. Moreover, a wealthy person never has money concerns. You may have millions of dollars in the bank, but if you think all the time about money, if you have concern about it, if you worry about it — about getting more, about not having enough, about losing it — then irrespective of the dollar amount you possess, you are poor.

To have true wealth or affluence is to be totally carefree about everything in life, including money. True wealth consciousness is, therefore, consciousness of the source of all material reality. This source of all material reality is pure consciousness. It is pure awareness. It is the unified field. It is the field of all possibilities.

THE A-TO-Z STEPS
TO A
RICHER LIFE

WHAT ARE THE STATES OF AWARENESS, the information and energy states that give rise to the experience of wealth in our lives?

For the sake of convenience, and to make it easy to remember, I have listed them in order as A-to-Z steps.

In my experience, it is not necessary to *consciously* practice the attitudes I am about to describe in order to materialize wealth. Using effort to consciously practice an attitude or to cultivate a mood is unnecessary and can cause stress and strain. It is important only that we know what these A-to-Z attitudes are, that we know what the steps are, that we be *aware* of them. The more we become aware of them, the more this knowledge gets structured in our consciousness and awareness. Then it is more likely that our attitude and behavior will change spontaneously, without any effort on our part.

Knowledge has organizing power inherent in it. It is simply enough to know, to be aware of the principles; the knowledge will be processed and metabolized by our bodies, and the results will be spontaneous. The results do not occur overnight, but begin to manifest gradually over a period of time.

If you will look at this list and read it once a day, or listen to it on tape every day, then you will see the changes that happen spontaneously in your life and the effortless ease with which wealth and affluence come into your life.

" A " STANDS FOR ALL POSSIBILITIES, absolute, authority, affluence, and abundance. The true nature of our ground state and that of the universe is that it is a field of all possibilities. In our most primordial form, we are a field of all possibilities.

From this level it is possible to create anything. This field is our own essential nature. It is our inner self.

It is also called the absolute, and it is the ultimate authority. It is intrinsically affluent because it gives rise to the infinite diversity and abundance of the universe.

"B" STANDS FOR BETTER AND BEST. Evolution implies getting better and better in every way with time, ultimately getting for ourselves the best of everything.

People with wealth consciousness settle only for the best. This is also called the principle of highest first. Go first class all the way and the universe will respond by giving you the best.

"C" STANDS FOR CAREFREENESS AND CHARITY.
A billion dollars in the bank, without
the experience of carefreeness and charity,
is a state of poverty. Wealth consciousness, by
definition, is a state of mind. If you are constantly concerned about how much money you
need, then irrespective of the actual dollar
amount you have in your account, you are
really poor.

Carefreeness automatically leads to charity and sharing because the source from
which it all comes is infinite, unbounded,
and inexhaustible.

"D" STANDS FOR THE LAW OF DEMAND and supply. Whatever service we are here to give, there is a demand for it. Ask yourself, "How may I serve?" and "How can I help?" The answers are within you. When you find those answers, you will also see and know that there is a demand for your service.

"D" also stands for dharma. Each of us has a dharma, a purpose in life. When we are in dharma, we enjoy and love our work.

"E" STANDS FOR EXULTING in the success of others, especially your competitors and those who consider themselves your enemies. Your competitors and enemies will become your helpers when you exult in their success.

"E" also stands for the principle that expectancy determines outcome. So always expect the best and you'll see that the outcome is spontaneously contained in the expectation.

"F" STANDS FOR THE FACT that in every failure is the seed of success. In the manifestation of the material from the non-material, of the visible from the invisible, a fundamental mechanics is involved. This is the principle of feedback.

Our failures are stepping-stones in the mechanics of creation, bringing us ever closer to our goals. In reality, there is no such thing as failure. What we call failure is just a mechanism through which we can learn to do things right.

"G" STANDS FOR GRATITUDE, generosity, God, gap, and goal. Gratitude and generosity are natural attributes of an affluent consciousness. Since the only thing to go after is the best, the principle of the highest first, why not adopt God as the role model? After all, no one is more affluent than God, for God is the field of all possibilities.

There is a precise mechanism through which all desires can be manifested. These four steps are as follows:

Step one: You slip into the gap between thoughts. The gap is the window, the corridor, the transformational vortex through which the personal psyche communicates with the cosmic psyche.

Step two: You have a clear intention of a clear goal in the gap.

Step three: You relinquish your attachment to the outcome, because chasing the outcome or getting attached to it entails coming out of the gap.

Step four: You let the universe handle the details.

It is important to have a clear goal in your awareness, but it is also important to relinquish your attachment to the goal. And the goal is in the gap, and the gap is the potentiality to organize and orchestrate the details required to affect any outcome.

Perhaps you recall an instant when you were trying to remember a name, and you struggled and struggled, but with no success. Finally, you let go of your attachment to the outcome, and then a little while later the name flashed across the screen of your consciousness. This is the mechanics for the fulfillment of any desire.

When you were struggling to recall the name, the mind was very active and turbulent. But ultimately, out of fatigue and frustration, you let go and the mind became quiet and slowly quieter — perhaps so quiet that it was almost still — and you slipped into the gap where you released your desire, and soon it was handed to you. This is the true meaning of "Ask and you shall receive," or "Knock and the door shall be opened to you."

One of the easiest and most effortless ways of slipping into the gap is through the process of meditation. And there are many forms of meditation and prayer that can help us to manifest desires from the level of the gap.

"H" STANDS FOR HAPPINESS and humanity and the fact that we are here to make all humans we come into contact with happy.

Life naturally evolves in the direction of happiness. We must constantly ask ourselves if what we are doing is going to make us, and those around us, happy. Because happiness is the ultimate goal. It is the goal of all other goals.

When we seek money, or a good relationship, or a great job, what we are really seeking is happiness. The mistake we make is not going for happiness first. If we did, everything else would follow.

"I" STANDS FOR THE POWER of unbending intent or intention. It is to make an unchangeable decision from which it is impossible to go back. It is singlemindedness of purpose.

In order to acquire wealth — or for that matter anything in the physical universe — you must intend it, make a decision to go for it. The decision is unchangeable with fixity of purpose, not countermanded by anything.

The universe handles the details, organizes and orchestrates opportunities. You have simply to be alert to these opportunities.

"J"
    STANDS FOR THE FACT that it is not necessary to judge. When we relinquish our need to constantly classify things as good or bad, right or wrong, then we experience more silence in our consciousness. Our internal dialogue begins to quieten when we shed the burden of judgment, and it is then easier to access the gap.

It is important, therefore, to get away from definitions, labels, descriptions, interpretations, evaluations, analyses, and judgment, for all of these create the turbulence of our internal dialogue.

"K" STANDS FOR THE FACT that organizing power is inherent in knowledge. Knowledge of any kind gets metabolized spontaneously and brings about a change in awareness from where it is possible to create new realities.

For example, becoming familiar with the knowledge in this book will spontaneously create the conditions for wealth and affluence.

"L" STANDS FOR LOVE AND LUXURY. Love yourself. Love your customers. Love your family. Love everybody. Love the world. There is no power stronger than love.

Also, adopt luxury as a lifestyle. Luxury is our natural state. Adopting luxury as a lifestyle sets the preamble, the preconditions for the flow of wealth.

"M" STANDS FOR MAKING MONEY for others and helping others make money. Helping others make money and helping other people to fulfill their desires is a sure way to ensure you'll make money for yourself as well as more easily fulfill your own dreams.

"M" also stands for motivate. The best way to motivate other people to help you fulfill your goals is to help them fulfill their goals.

"N" STANDS FOR SAYING NO to negativity. My friend Wayne Dyer, the famous author, taught me a simple technique for this. Whenever he has a negative thought he silently says to himself, "Next," and moves on.

Saying no to negativity also means not being around negative people. Negative people deplete your energy. Surround yourself with love and nourishment and do not allow the creation of negativity in your environment.

"**O**" STANDS FOR THE FACT that life is the coexistence of all opposite values. Joy and sorrow, pleasure and pain, up and down, hot and cold, here and there, light and darkness, birth and death. All experience is by contrast, and one would be meaningless without the other.

A wise seer once said, "A man born blind from birth will never know the meaning of darkness because he has never experienced light."

When there is a quiet reconciliation, an acceptance in our awareness of this lively coexistence of all opposite values, then automatically we become more and more nonjudgmental.

The victor and the vanquished are seen as two poles of the same being. Nonjudgment leads to quietening of the internal dialogue, and this opens the doorway to creativity.

"O" also stands for opportunity and open and honest communication. Every contact with every human being is an opportunity for growth and the fulfillment of desire — one has only to be alert to the opportunities through increased awareness. Open and honest communication opens the channels to realize those opportunities.

"P" STANDS FOR PURPOSE IN LIFE and for pure potentiality. We are here to fulfill a purpose. It is up to us to find out what that purpose is. Once we know our purpose then the knowledge of one's purpose leads to the insight that we are true potentiality.

We must be able to state our purpose in very simple terms. For example, my purpose in life is to heal, to make everyone I come into contact with happy, and to create peace.

Knowing our purpose opens up the doorway to the field of pure potentiality because inherent in our desire are the seeds and mechanics for its fulfillment.

"Q" IS TO QUESTION: to question dogma, question ideology, question outside authority. It is only by questioning what people take for granted, what people hold to be true, that we can break through the hypnosis of social conditioning.

"R" STANDS FOR THE FACT that receiving is as necessary as giving. To graciously receive is an expression of the dignity of giving. Those who are unable to receive are actually incapable of giving. Giving and receiving are different aspects of the flow of energy in the universe; they do not have to be in the form of material things.

To graciously receive a compliment or admiration or respect also implies the ability to be able to give these to others. And absence of respect, courtesy, manners, or admiration creates a state of poverty irrespective of the amount of money you have in the bank.

"**S**"
STANDS FOR SPENDING AND SERVICE. Money
is like blood; it must flow. Hoarding and hold-
ing on to it causes sludging. In order to grow,
it must flow. Otherwise it gets blocked and, like
clotted blood, it can only cause damage.

Money is life energy that we exchange and
use as a result of the service we provide to the
universe. And in order to keep it coming to us,
we must keep it circulating.

"T" STANDS FOR TRANSCENDENCE, timeless awareness, talent bank, and tithing. My personal experience is that without transcendence, life has no beauty. My experience of transcendence through the practice of meditation gives me an inner stability and silence that is not overshadowed by any activity. That silence stays with me so that no outer experience can overshadow the awareness and experience of the self.

"T" also stands for timeless awareness, as opposed to time-bound awareness. Time-bound awareness occurs when we relinquish the self for the self-image. The self-image is the social mask, the protective veneer behind which we hide. In time-bound awareness our behavior is always influenced by the past and by anticipation and fear of the future. It is burdened by guilt and sorrow; it is rooted in fear. Timeless awareness is the awareness of the self. The self is not in the realm of thought. It's in the gap between our thoughts. This is also what we call intuition. Time-bound awareness is in the intellect; it calculates. Timeless awareness is in the heart; it feels.

"T" also stands for talent bank. In order to maximize creativity and offer the best service, it is good to develop a talent bank or a coterie of individuals with unique and diverse talents and abilities and whose individual talents, when added together, are more than the sum of the parts.

"T" also stands for tithing. Tithing means giving away a certain portion of your income without conditions or strings attached. When you give, a vacuum is created that attracts even more of what you have given away.

"U" STANDS FOR UNDERSTANDING the unity behind all diversity. Unity consciousness is a state of enlightenment where we pierce the mask of illusion which creates separation and fragmentation. Behind the appearance of separation is one unified field of wholeness. Here the seer and the scenery are one.

We experience unity consciousness when we are in love, when we are with nature gazing at the stars or walking on the beach, listening to music, dancing, reading poetry, praying, and in the silence of meditation.

In unity consciousness, we slip through the barrier of time into the playground of eternity.

"**V**"
STANDS FOR VALUES: truth, integrity, honesty, love, faith, devotion, and beauty. The great Indian poet Rabindranath Tagore says, "When we feel beauty, we know it as truth."

Without values, there is confusion and chaos. When values disintegrate everything disintegrates. Health disintegrates, poverty attains dominance over affluence, societies and civilizations crumble.

When we pay attention to these values that society has always held sacred, then order emerges out of chaos, and the field of pure potentiality inside us becomes all-powerful, creating anything it desires.

"W"

STANDS FOR WEALTH consciousness without worries. Wealth consciousness implies
absence of money worries. Truly wealthy people
never worry about losing their money because
they know that wherever money comes from
there is an inexhaustible supply of it.

Once, when we were discussing a world
peace project with my teacher, Maharishi
Mahesh Yogi, somebody asked him, "Where is
all the money going to come from?" And he
replied without hesitation, "From wherever it is
at the moment."

"X"

X STANDS FOR EXPRESSING honest appreciation and thanks to all who help us. We must never pretend appreciation, but if we feel it, then we must express it. The expression of gratitude is a powerful force that generates even more of what we have already received.

"**Y**" STANDS FOR YOUTHFUL VIGOR. We experience health when our identity of who we are comes from reference to the self. When we identify with objects, whether these are situations, circumstances, people, or things, then we relinquish our energy to the object of reference. As a result, we feel lack of energy and vitality.

When our identity comes from the self, then we keep our energy to ourselves. We feel energetic, we feel powerful, and we experience youthful vigor.

"Z" STANDS FOR ZEST FOR LIFE. It is to appreciate life in all its vitality and exuberance. It is to know that there is only one life that expresses itself in myriad forms. To see that life is to know that power is in the present moment. It is to know that I am that, that you are that, that all this is that, and that's all there is.

Tagore once said, "The same stream of life that runs through the world runs through my veins night and day and dances in rhythmic measure. It is the same life that shoots in joy through the dust of the earth into numberless blades of grass and breaks into tumultuous waves of flowers." He calls this "the life throb of ages, dancing in my blood this moment." To be in touch with this life throb of ages dancing in our blood this moment, is to have zest for life. It is to face the unknown with carefreeness and freedom.

The unknown is the field of all possibilities in every moment of the present. And this is freedom, beyond the known of past conditioning, beyond the prison of space, time, and causation.

As Don Juan once said to Carlos Castaneda, "It does not matter what our specific fate is, as long as we face it with ultimate abandon." This is carefreeness. This is joy. This is freedom. This is zest for life.

S O THERE YOU ARE. These are the stepping-stones to unlimited wealth, the A-to-Z of prosperity. Once again, you do not need to consciously cultivate a mood of these attributes. You need only to be aware of them. Read the list daily, or just listen to it on tape, and you will see your life change and become an expression of affluence, of unboundedness, abundance, infinity, and immortality.

Create as much wealth as your heart desires. Fulfill every material and non-material desire. Create wealth and spend it. Spend it lavishly and then share it and give it to others. Give it to your children, to your family, to your relatives, to your friends, to society, and to the world. For wealth is of the universe and it does not belong to us — we belong to it.

We are privileged children and the universe has chosen to share its bounty with us. We only have to give our attention to affluence and it will be ours.

ABOUT THE AUTHOR

*D*EEPAK CHOPRA, M.D. is a pioneer in the field of mind-body medicine and human potential and the best-selling author of *Ageless Body*, *Timeless Mind* and *Quantum Healing*. His groundbreaking works blend physics and philosophy, the practical and the spiritual, venerable Eastern wisdom and cutting-edge Western science with dynamic results.

The A-to-Z steps are taken from chapter two of
*Creating Affluence: Wealth Consciousness
in the Field of All Possibilities*

The complete 112-page volume of
Creating Affluence is available in a beautiful
hardcover gift edition. Exquisitely designed with
two-color printing throughout, this keepsake
volume is a lifelong companion, destined to be
read and referred to again and again.

Hardcover Gift Edition ÷ $12.95
Audio Cassette ÷ $11.95

To order the complete book and audio cassette, or
for a free catalog of our fine products, contact:

New World Library
58 Paul Drive, Dept. 194
San Rafael, California 94903

Phone: (415) 472-2100 ÷ Fax: (415) 472-6131
Or call toll-free:
(800) 227-3900

Also from
Deepak Chopra, M.D.

Books

Ageless Body, Timeless Mind. Crown.

Unconditional Life: Discovering the Power to Fulfill Your Dreams. Bantam.

Perfect Health: The Complete Mind-Body Guide. Crown.

Quantum Healing: Exploring the Frontiers of Mind-Body Medicine. Bantam.

Return of the Rishi: A Doctor's Story of Spiritual Transformation & Ayurvedic Healing. Houghton Mifflin.

Creating Health: How to Wake Up the Body's Intelligence. Houghton Mifflin.

Audio Cassettes

Escaping the Prison of the Intellect: A Journey from Here to Here. New World Library.

Living Beyond Miracles (with Dr. Wayne Dyer). New World Library.

Sacred Verses, Healing Sounds. New World Library.